Berry Good Time

It is 4 o'clock!

Strawberry Shortcake and her friends have a berry good time around the clock. Let's learn about time as we go through Strawberryland.

The long hand shows the minutes. It is called the **minute hand**.

The short hand shows the hour. It is called the **hour hand**.

Trace the **hour hand**.

Trace the **minute hand**.

Trace the numbers on the clock's face.

It is 1 o'clock in Strawberryland!

Trace and draw hands to show **1 o'clock**.

Strawberry Shortcake jumps rope at 1:00 in the afternoon!

1 o'clock is also written as 1:00. Trace and write **1:00**.

Berry fun!

Do you jump rope?

It is 2 o'clock in Strawberryland!

Trace and draw hands to show **2 o'clock**.

2 o'clock is also written as 2:00. Trace and write **2:00**.

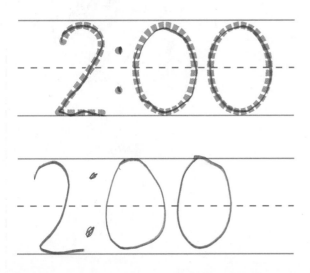

Apple Dumplin' has a snack at 2:00 in the afternoon!

Sweet Stuff!

What snacks do you like?

It is 3 o'clock in Strawberryland!

Trace and draw hands to show **3 o'clock**.

3 o'clock is also written as 3:00. Trace and write **3:00**.

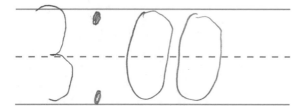

Strawberry Shortcake roller skates at 3:00 in the afternoon!

Going where the fun is!

Do you roller skate?

Trace and draw hands to show **4 o'clock**.

Strawberry Shortcake flies a kite at 4:00 in the afternoon!

4 o'clock is also written as 4:00. Trace and write **4:00**.

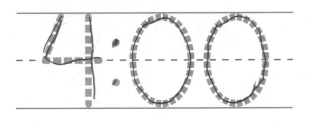

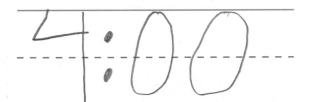

Fun day!

Did you ever fly a kite?

It is 5 o'clock in Strawberryland!

Trace and draw hands to show **5 o'clock**.

5 o'clock is also written as 5:00. Trace and write **5:00**.

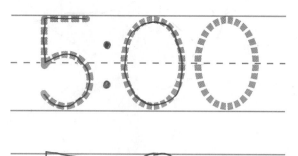

Strawberry Shortcake does ballet at 5:00 in the evening!

So cute!

What do you do at 5:00?

It is 6 o'clock in Strawberryland!

Trace and draw hands to show **6 o'clock**.

6 o'clock is also written as 6:00. Trace and write **6:00**.

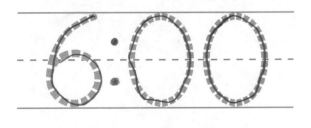

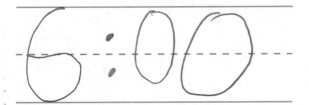

Huckleberry Pie skateboards at 6:00 in the evening!

Cool kid!

Do you have a skateboard?

Trace and draw hands to show **7 o'clock**.

7 o'clock is also written as 7:00. Trace and write **7:00**.

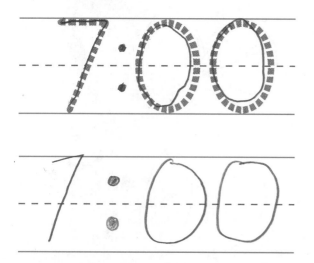

Strawberry Shortcake gets dressed at 7:00 in the morning!

What is your favorite outfit?

Trace and draw hands to show **8 o'clock**.

8 o'clock is also written as 8:00. Trace and write **8:00**.

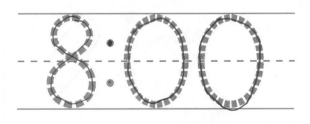

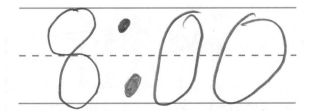

Strawberry Shortcake eats breakfast at 8:00 in the morning!

What do you eat for breakfast?

It is 9 o'clock in Strawberryland!

Trace and draw hands to show **9 o'clock**.

9 o'clock is also written as 9:00. Trace and write **9:00**.

9:00

9:00

Strawberry Shortcake waters plants at 9:00 in the morning!

Growing better every day!

Do you have any plants?

Trace and draw hands to show **10 o'clock**.

10 o'clock is also written as 10:00. Trace and write **10:00**.

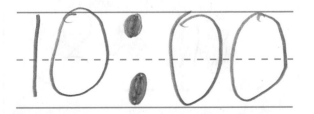

Angel Cake bakes a cake at 10:00 in the morning!

Life is sweet!

Do you help bake cakes?

It is 11 o'clock in Strawberryland!

Trace and draw hands to show **11 o'clock**.

11 o'clock is also written as 11:00. Trace and write **11:00**.

Strawberry Shortcake takes a walk at 11:00 in the morning!

My berry best sister!

When do you go for walk?

It is 12 o'clock in Strawberryland!

Trace and draw hands to show **12 o'clock**.

The minute hand covers up the hour hand at 12:00!

12 o'clock is also written as 12:00. Trace and write **12:00**.

12:00

12:00

Strawberry Shortcake eats lunch at 12:00 noon!

It's all good!

What do you eat for lunch?

13

Berry Fruity

Strawberry Shortcake can tell time to the hour. Can you? Circle the correct time below each clock.

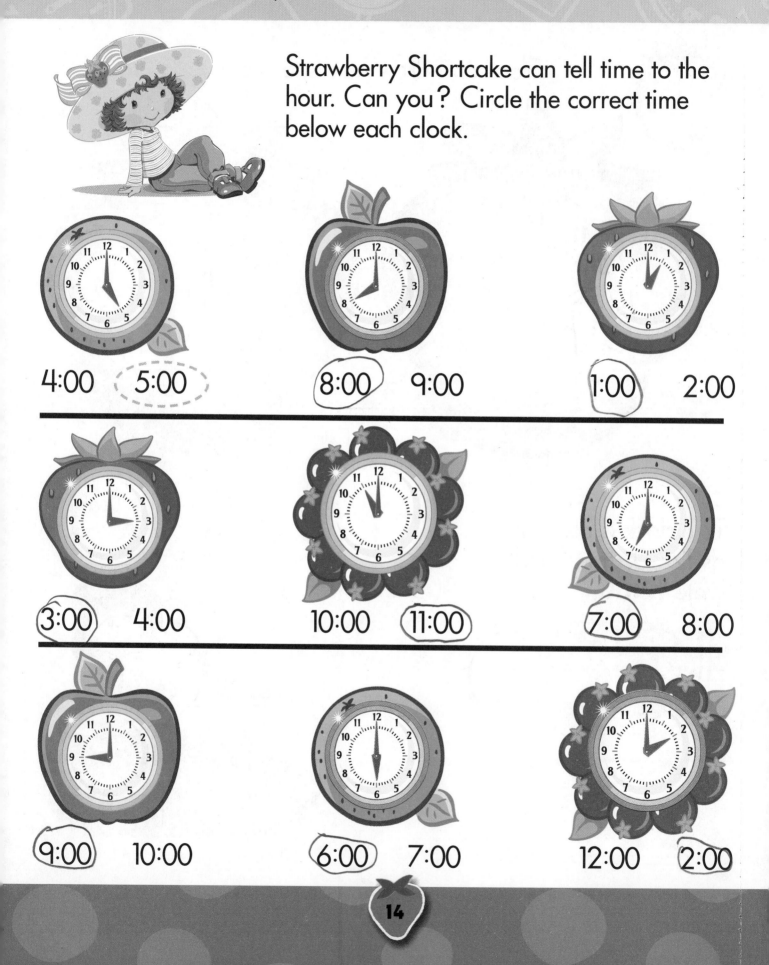

4:00   (5:00)

(8:00)   9:00

(1:00)   2:00

(3:00)   4:00

10:00   (11:00)

(7:00)   8:00

(9:00)   10:00

(6:00)   7:00

12:00   (2:00)

Flower Power

Show your flower power. Draw hands on each clock to show the correct time.

10:00

4:00

12:00

6:00

9:00

11:00

Trace and draw hands to show **half past 1**.

Half past 1 is also written as 1:30.
Trace and write **1:30**.

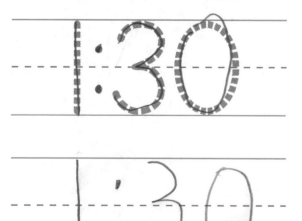

Strawberry Shortcake rides Honey Pie at 1:30 in the afternoon!

On my way to a happy day!

Did you ever ride a pony?

Trace and draw hands to show **half past 2**.

Half past 2 is also
written as 2:30.
Trace and write **2:30**.

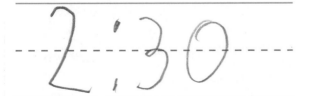

Ginger Snap bakes cookies
at 2:30 in the afternoon!

Delish!

What's your favorite cookie?

Trace and draw hands to show **half past 3**.

Half past 3 is also
written as 3:30.
Trace and write **3:30**.

Strawberry Shortcake decorates
cookies at 3:30 in the afternoon!

Sweetest of
the sweet!

Do you decorate cookies?

It is half past 4 in Strawberryland!

Trace and draw hands to show **half past 4**.

Half past 4 is also written as 4:30.
Trace and write **4:30**.

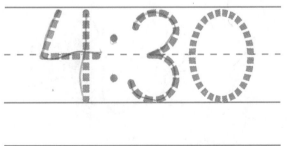

Blueberry Muffin dances at 4:30 in the afternoon!

Sweet and sassy!

Do you like to dance?

Trace and draw hands to show **half past 5**.

Half past 5 is also written as 5:30.
Trace and write **5:30**.

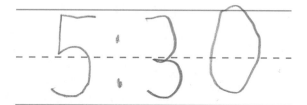

Strawberry Shortcake plays with Pupcake at 5:30 in the evening!

Sweetest of the sweet!

Do you have a pet?

It is half past 6 in Strawberryland!

Trace and draw hands to show **half past 6**.

Half past 6 is also written as 6:30.
Trace and write **6:30**.

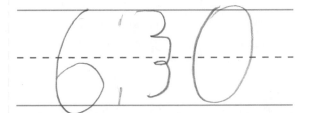

Strawberry Shortcake eats supper at 6:30 in the evening.

What time do you eat supper?

It is half past 7 in Strawberryland!

Trace and draw hands to show **half past 7**.

Half past 7 is also written as 7:30.
Trace and write **7:30**.

7:30

7:30

Strawberry Shortcake reads at 7:30 in the evening!

This is a berry good book!

When do you read?

It is half past 8 in Strawberryland!

Trace and draw hands to show **half past 8**.

Half past 8 is also written as 8:30.
Trace and write **8:30**.

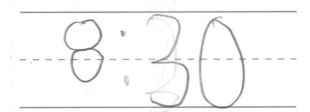

Strawberry Shortcake rides her scooter at 8:30 in the morning.

Berry cool!

Do you have a scooter?

It is half past 9 in Strawberryland!

Trace and draw hands to show **half past 9**.

Half past 9 is also written as 9:30.
Trace and write **9:30**.

9:30

Strawberry Shortcake swims at 9:30 in the morning!

My favorite day is fun day!

Can you swim?

It is half past 10 in Strawberryland!

Trace and draw hands to show **half past 10**.

Half past 10 is also written as 10:30.
Trace and write **10:30**.

$$10:30$$

Orange Blossom cheers at 10:30 in the morning!

Be you!

How loudly can you cheer?

It is half past 11 in Strawberryland!

Trace and draw hands to show **half past 11**.

Half past 11 is also written as 11:30.
Trace and write **11:30**.

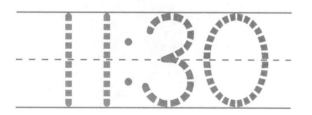

Strawberry Shortcake swings at 11:30 in the morning!

Glad to be me!

Do you like to swing?

It is half past 12 in Strawberryland!

Trace and draw hands to show **half past 12**.

Half past 12 is also written as 12:30.
Trace and write **12:30**.

Strawberry Shortcake eats ice cream at 12:30 in the afternoon!

Life is delicious!

What's your favorite ice cream?

Time Flies

Strawberry Shortcake can tell time to the half hour. Can you? Circle the correct time below each clock.

(1:30)   2:30

6:30   7:30

3:30   4:30

9:30   10:30

2:30   3:30

8:30   9:30

11:30   12:30

9:30   8:30

5:30   6:30

More Flower Power

Show how much you've grown.
Draw hands on each clock to show the correct time.

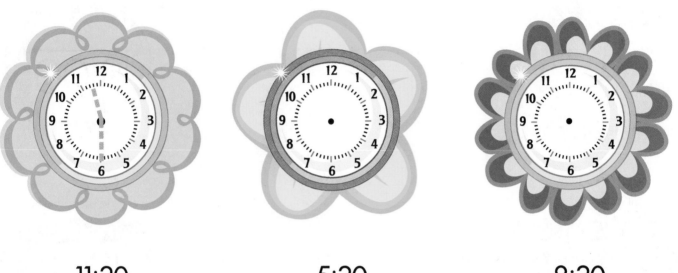

11:30   5:30   8:30

10:30   12:30   4:30

Berry Good Match

Strawberry Shortcake spends hours picking strawberries.
Draw lines to match the strawberries with the same time.

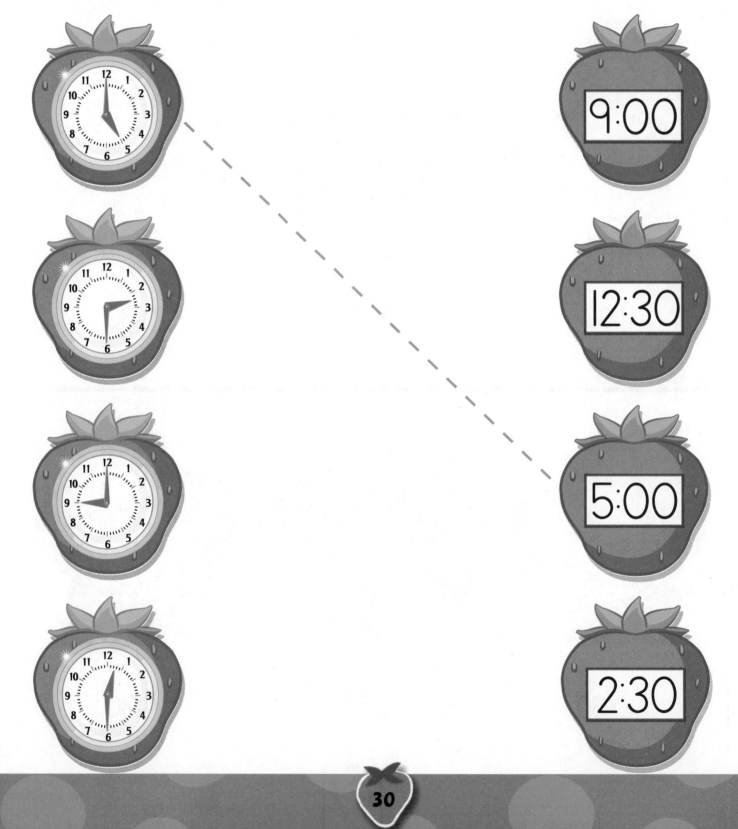

It's time for new shoes. Draw lines from the ponies to the horseshoe clocks with the same time.

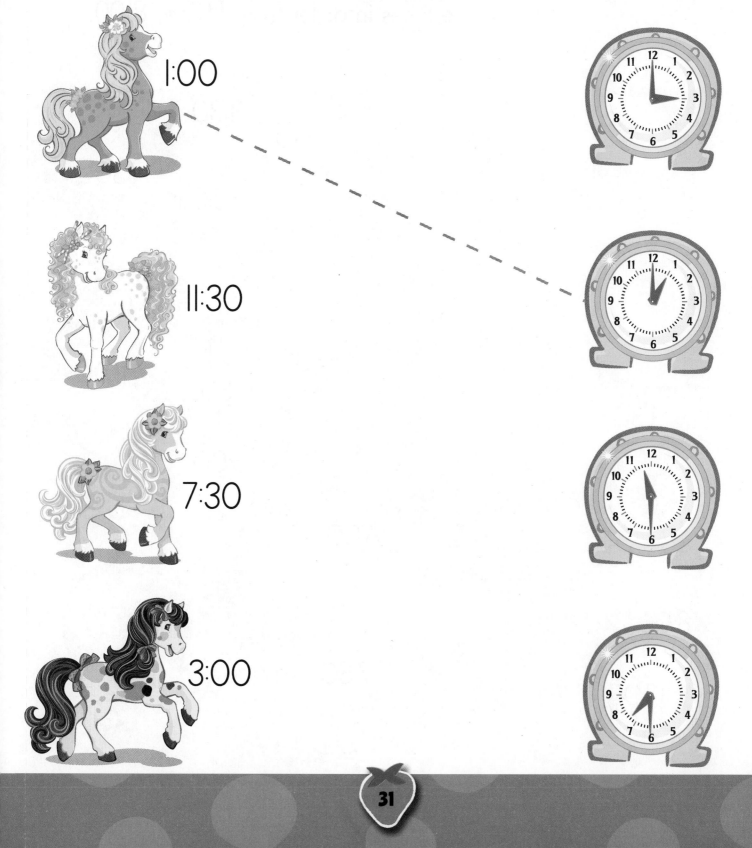

1:00

11:30

7:30

3:00

Time to Go Home

Help Strawberry Shortcake get home to her berry bungalow. Draw a line along the path that shows the times in order from 1:00 to 8:00.

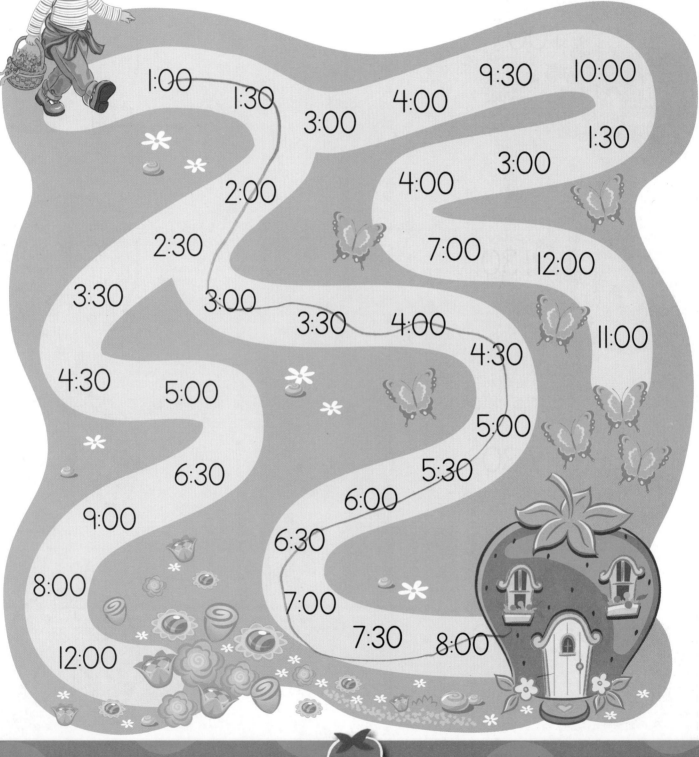